# Vanishing Below the Waist

*Winner of the Heartland Review Chapbook contest, finalist in the Wolfson Press Chapbook Competition & Two Sylvias Press Chapbook Contest, semi-finalist for Yellow Arrow Publishing's Chapbook Contest, shortlisted for Galileo Press Chapbook contest, & longlisted for The Rachel Wetzseon Chapbook Award*

# ALSO BY ELLIE WHITE

*and for too long after*
*Drift*
*Requiem for a Doll*

# *Vanishing Below the Waist*

## *Ellie White*

QUERENCIA

*Querencia Press – Chicago IL*

QUERENCIA PRESS

© Copyright 2024
**Ellie White**

ISBN 978 1 959118 86 2


www.querenciapress.com


First Published in 2024

**Querencia Press, LLC**
**Chicago IL**

Printed & Bound in the United States of America

"Imagine a ruin so strange it must never have happened."

—Barbara Kingsolver, *The Poisonwood Bible*

# CONTENTS

# ONE

**Everything is so okay**[1]

you decide to bake cookies for everyone
you know and pretend they are not apologies.
you try to look your partner in the eyes
during sex because you know he likes it.
try to hide your revulsion. you do need him,
after all, and need is almost like love.
you resolve to start running again.
ignore the rusty gate in your chest
for a quarter mile. cough for the next 2 days.
this is called grit. you no longer cry
in the shower. blame the callous cement floor.
weary relic of gentler days when women
didn't cry in their showers, didn't cry at all
for fear of ruining their complexions.
your complexion is already ruined.
what the fuck are you trying to save?

---

[1] Inspired by *Nothing is Okay* by Rachel Wiley

**Eden**

Eve's new weight bends her head
heavy. The sea-green trees
edge teal, then grey. Their leaves:
empty shells. They remember
her serene eyes, her gentle
breath. Beneath them, Eve weeps,
bleeds a new sea. The red earth
peals, then peels. The sea
seeps ever-deeper, ever-redder.
Even heaven gets wrecked.

**Dyspareunia / Genesis**

Once there was a knife / Once my body was a river
        that became a slick fish / that begat a dull ache
                that became a paper wasp / that begat a sharpness
                        that became a fire / that begat shadows
                that became sand
        that became glass
                that became a fist
                        that became rebar / that begat a scream
                that became a meteor / that begat buzzing
                        that became an explosion / that begat silence
                that became a crater / that begat a new mattress
that became *stop*
        that became *I'm sorry*
                that became *no more*
                        that became salt / that begat a wound
        that became a whisper / that begat two six-packs
                that became white ducks / that begat a riverbank
                        that became a pillow / that begat a moonless sky

**Vulvodynia**

Here is bramble and thorn, stinging asp
and copperhead, alder tree and swamp.
Here, the shreds of my first love strung
on a low hanging branch. Here, the ashes of
a love I wasn't allowed poured into a thousand
yellow jacket nests. Here is buzz and sting,
swell and ache, burn and burn. Not pictured:
his sweet, shocked face as I pulled away
from his kiss. How it is always rising
up from the murky water. He resurrects
and resurrects. And each time,
I know again that this is my fault.

**Endometrioma**

I found out I was pregnant the same day
I had my daughter. This seemed normal.
I drove to the hospital where I screamed,
cried, and pushed until she was screaming
back. Her name was Angelica Danielle:
a honey blonde, lapis-eyed wonder with skin
like apricot blossoms. There were important
decisions to make. I worried breastfeeding
would hurt too much. Stood in front
of shelves stocked with dozens of formulas.
Thrilled to find it came in chocolate,
like ice cream. Surely, she'd eat it.

At home, I paced the floor night and day,
Angelica Danielle in my arms like a sleeping
bomb. Sleep: something I no longer did.
I used to wrap her in blankets printed
with moons, stars, planets. My galaxy child.
Keeper of comets and space dust. Ignorer
of all lullabies, except the one about horses[2].

I awoke in the dark smelling baby formula
and pictured it: a chocolate-colored apricot
growing from the bud of my left ovary,
sucking the life out of what could be life.

---

[2] "All the Pretty Little Horses"

**Vanishing Below the Waist**

*—Union Station, Washington D.C.*

Standing in line
to get off the train,
the door separating
this car from its siblings
closes against my hip.
Smoking behind a pillar
by the tour buses,
a bold brindled bird
pecks my boot. As I perch
in a metal cubicle,
the automatic toilet flushes
itself beneath me. I glance
down at the pale blue panties
stretched ungracefully
across my thighs,
and see five dark hairs
have been ripped out,
the bulb-like follicles
still attached. I wonder
how I did not feel this.

## Street Corner Mermaid

*—For the mermaids of Norfolk, Virginia*

When the river gathers itself like the behemoth
slug it is, and lurches forward over the bank.
When it fills the streets to the curb and keeps rising.
When children gleefully begin kayaking around
their front yards. Then, I am home.

Seaweed, croaker, muskrat. In the murky swell,
they surround me. I dream of rusty propeller
blades, scrap metal, dead trees. Anything large
enough to smash this pedestal I've been glued to.
Left to rot in the sun year after year.

To fade, to crack, to rust. My arm fell off again.
I heard a father tell his child the city can't pay
to put it back. He said I am still pretty
this way. Beauty comes in many forms.
Nor-Easter, hurricane, bomb cyclone, many forms.

**What I Mean**

When I say don't touch me, what I mean is you don't want to touch me.

When I say you wouldn't understand, I mean I don't want you to.

When I say explaining hurts too much, I mean it has taken me thirteen years to shove an elephant into a pillowcase, make the beast small enough to slip under my shirt.

When I say I will never really be able to let you in, I mean I cannot sleep with you. Not that I will not, but that I cannot.

When I say nothing happened to me, I mean I am not a survivor.

When I say I am done with doctors, I mean I am done hurting. No more jars of instant rug burn. No more needles full of wasps. No more praying to two inches of lukewarm water in the bathtub.

When I say I believe everything happens for a reason, I mean there is no fucking reason, and I will throw every knife in the house at the mere suggestion of one.

When I ask you not to say you're sorry, I mean a person can die of sympathy.

When I say, again, don't touch me, I mean what is left of me is fanged and feral.

When I say it is too soon for a cure, too soon to even be sure of the diagnosis, I mean there are still legions of the afflicted biting screams back into our tongues as our lovers struggle to enter us.

As our bodies revolt, as they have every time this year: this decade: this life, we are still quietly apologizing as the elephant crushes us to death.

# *TWO*

**Strawberry Fields Forever**[3]

I can't say that I'm not a strawberry,
bright and vacant in my candied cadmium
skin, lying alone on the asphalt of Park Street.
I may have been dropped, but not squashed,
by any of these good, healthy people walking
by in their Patagonia and Keens. I can't say
that I'm not organic. I may be nutritious
but also laced with pesticide. Is my red too red
to be natural? I can't say that I'm not seeded,
not crowned with bitter green leaves. That is,
I think I disagree. I don't believe I once sat
in a green plastic basket in an open market
in Liverpool where a tourist purchased me,
took me up to her hostel bunk bed and sucked my
insides through her teeth. I don't think she drank
a small bottle of white wine and fell asleep
still holding my crown in her hand.

---

[3] This poem borrows its title and one line from The Beatles

**Poem in Which I Cure Myself of Binge Drinking**

I hand myself a glass of pink
lemonade more satisfying
than the smoothest red blend,
sweetest Moscato, driest
Sauvignon Blanc. From now on,
I will want nothing else.
The smell of a G&T will turn
my stomach. Belgian white ale
will evoke piss or dirty dishwater.
I'll find myself hovering
over the citrus fruits at Kroger,
trying to choose the perfect
hue and firmness for tonight's meal.

In the morning, a half-full flute:
blushing tulip with translucent leaves,
rests quietly on my nightstand,
all that lingers from the night before.

**A Personal History of Bruxism**

What nobody tells you about fillings is they crack.
Even if you brush in perfect little circles, avoid sugar
before bed, it will happen. Gurgle warm salt
water, rub your gums with clove oil, Google chimes
in with advice. On the way to the dentist, school bells
ringing all the way. Jammed in a minivan traffic legacy.

Bad teeth run in your family, a dental legacy
to match the psychological. Orthodontia and minds crack
similarly. The surprise of biting a metal fork. Bells
and whistles. A melody of sirens. Too much sugar.
At least you have a Twinkie defense. Ding Dongs chime
in the key of Is It Over? You taste dimes and salt.

Your sister got veneers because the Smiths didn't salt
their driveway. It was veneers or a legacy
of broken bonds. Your mom was so quick to chime
in her support. The gilded guilt about to crack
her wide open. You remember snow like sugar
dust across the ice. The radio playing Jingle Bells.

In your house, the cats have no bells.
You learned to pry them off with pliers. No salt
on Mom's popcorn. No cinnamon. Just sugar
in the cookies. A never-ending legacy
of how she likes things. Dad's on crack
and one of the damn neighbors got a windchime.

You buy a special alarm clock. No chimes,
buzzers, beeps, or banging church bells.
You wake up to ocean waves because crack
isn't the joke it used to be. You still cut salt
like coke at Cici's Pizza, laugh loud like your legacy
depends on it. Your teeth start to dissolve like sugar.

Fourteen years old, the dentist says Less sugar
and Do you make yourself throw up? Two chimes
to his office. Five to the shrinks. Adolescence a legacy
whispered in elevator shafts. Mute the alarm bells
as you slip past statistics. Please hold the salt.
Hold yourself still. Plummet through every crack.

Grind your teeth to sugar. Hollow as bells
inside, they chime a song of cuts and salt.
A teenage tragedy, a legacy, of all the ways to crack.

**The Spectacle of Craving**

I go to the kitchen to fill my glass
of wine and leave my body
along the way. Her feet make no sound
on the rug except when she stumbles
over an old cat toy. It jingles away
under the bookcase. The lights flicker
on the Christmas tree as she passes.
Each silent step: another drop
into a perfectly round bowl,
the bright crystal swelling with
Sauvignon Blanc. The kitchen's cool
linoleum glides beneath her socks.
She's arrived but the glass has vanished.
I'm holding a knife.
In my other hand, an orange.

**Poem Ending in an Apology to Something Recently Deceased**

*I'm just trying to make you*
*laugh* the strange, older man
at the Exxon station shouts at me
over two aisles sparsely stocked
with chips, candy, wiper fluid,
and overpriced Tylenol. I barely
look up, so he shouts it again, louder.

I give him a nervous smile, an *okay, sir*
as I head to the register with my longneck
can of cider. The cashier and I both
ignore the man as he attempts to pay
for my drink. The front door slams.
He storms off to his car.

I needed another drink
because my good friend found out
today that her dog is going to die.
*Some kind of cancer. Only a few*
*weeks*. And I'm sad for her, sad
for the dog. But also reminded
of my own cat who's dying,
which is a loss I can't accept.

As I'm walking home, I can see
something dark along the edge
of the right lane. A thing I don't
recall being there five minutes ago.

I wait for a car, for its headlights
to reveal the object. Asphalt,
yellow line, pool of shiny, dark liquid,
pink nose, whiskers, glassy eyes.

I walk by at first. But I know
it's still in the lane. It could belong
to someone. I have to turn around.
I shove the longneck can into the pouch
of my hoodie. I need the plastic bag.
I wait for all the cars to pass, willing
each one not to run over the corpse.

Using the bag as a glove, I gently grab
the middle of the tail, drag the small,
still warm, soft body to the curb.
With my plastic-sheathed hand,
I stroke the cat's fluffy back just once,
whisper *I'm sorry. I'm so, so sorry.*

**The day before I turn thirty-five**

my mother is suddenly afraid
I'll drown in the lake behind her house.
She tells me this in the kitchen
as I'm preparing to lay out on the dock.
I see her seeing me underwater.
I've hit my head. Blood billows out
from the wound, fades into the green-
brown water. I'm unconscious. Suspended
just below the surface. Face down.
No. Face up. Like a horror movie.
Tiny bubbles of air trickle from my nose
as my lungs fill with water: veiny, purple
balloons. Mom will look out the window.
I'll be gone. She'll panic, searching
the deserted dock. My book, my phone,
my sunscreen, my towel, but where am I?
A boat will drive by, the dock creaking as its wake
rolls towards shore. And I'll surface for a split
second at the same time Mom's looking down
into the lake: a mannequin of myself with a red
halo. As Mom puts sunscreen on my back,
she asks *Where can you touch the bottom
out there?* and I answer *Nowhere.*

**Narthex**

At the meeting, the man next to me is searching
for a more potent word for chaos. I offer *mayhem*.
He continues his personal reflection as I stare
at the floral rug. The flowers could be crustaceans
or vulvas. I see the carved piece of rose quartz
I impulse bought from a pregnant friend.
Someone else ordered this curious crystal,
but failed to pick it up or pay for it. My friend,
the seller, was modest. The delicately layered
labia and tiny bulge of clitoris embarrassed her.
I deemed her relief worth my forty dollars
plus shipping. We are passing the basket now.
Next, we will all stand and pray to a god
who is not of my choosing. I won't say the prayer
aloud. Instead, I'll picture myself in the shower
this morning—gripped by a sudden shockwave
of mortifying memories—and wonder who
I was begging in the steam to take it all away.

# *THREE*

**Dream Lover**

Every night, the moon wraps me
in a space blanket and appoints
a star to tell me a story.
The moon stays awake until
I fall asleep. The moon strokes
my hair, tells me my eyes look like
comets. I can squeeze the moon
as hard as I want. It never complains.

The moon doesn't drift away
from me when I'm sad.
It can withstand my weight
even when I'm heavy as a planet.
The moon teaches me how to
change a tire, fix a dripping sink,
light a campfire. It never asks
about my parents. It just listens.

## Blue Mud Dauber

The wasp, a thread-waisted beauty,
her metallic blue-black body shimmering
as she bounces around the light
bulb in the bathroom, is too much.

Nude and blinded by bug spray, I run
screaming across the one-room efficiency.
Crouched in the corner, for the first time
in our 18-month relationship, I call him.

He picks up and my frantic sobs slingshot
from tower to tower. It takes forty-one minutes.
His voice coaxes me to flush my eyes, wash
my face, and find something to wear.

He guides me back to the bathroom where
a detached wing glitters on the linoleum.
My cats have cornered her. Watching her die
is the second hardest thing I've done today.

## Unclogging the Shower Drain

I plunge my good eyebrow tweezers
down as deep as they will go, poking
them around in the dark. Mercilessly,
I yank sticky clumps of hair and wax
from the drain of a shower that is not mine.
Most of the hair is not mine. It belongs
to the many women and men who use
this house to live out their kinky fantasies,
then rinse off the evidence, be it blood,
sweat, or wax, here in the extra bathroom.

The house is full of whips, but its owner
is no leather-clad Master, no muscle-
bound Dom with a chiseled silhouette.
My orgasms last night were mediocre,
his fingers enormous sausages with nails
that needed clipping. The first man
I let touch my pussy in seven years
had chubby fingers, a soft gut, gray hair.
I ground myself against his hand anyway,
and in the morning, the shower.

**Ode to Bathing on My Period**

God love the once yellow wood
paneling, the black fauna beneath
each warped beige strip. Praise be
to cracked tile, chipped squares barely
clinging to grout, a few just set
in place, held by hope. Glory
to this ancient tub and all four
of its clawed feet, how they brace
the rusted-out bottom: a low, brown sky
snowing red ash. Lord bless the warmth
of the water, my body half-submerged,
my toes and breasts: islands. And
fluttering around this archipelago of flesh,
a sacred swarm of ruby jellyfish,
their emergence temporarily painless.

**Poem in Which I Expand**

I secret glitter into him,

        galaxy everything I touch.

                Sprinkle sparkles in his undershirts,

    socks, boxer briefs. Lace his bath towel,

all the clean pillowcases. I don't stop

                  until every surface is coated,

              till everything in his house is a part of me.

We fuck, and I'm the only one

        to get off. He observes me

from the end of the bed, a scientist seeking

    the source of all this dark energy.

                    I thrust my hips against the air,

              a jeweled plug winking between my cheeks.

     He finds silver stars

        in his pubes for weeks. He says

                *You are everywhere.* I say *Thank you.*

**Prophecy: A Recipe**

You'll need a fish and some sequins,
a bottle of good wine, sugar,
rock salt, a bag of mints, and maybe
an orange or two. This is not
a comprehensive list. Improvise a bit.
If it were meant to be simple, anyone
could do it. Are you still listening to me?
Good. Now you need to build a boat.
Not a real boat, an imaginary boat.
Exactly 12 feet and 4 inches long.
It should smell like pine trees
in your boat. You must stack coins
edge to edge. Bind them with candy
floss. It doesn't matter what color.
It just needs to be sticky. You have
too many questions. Why would I know
when the flood is coming? Who said
it would end in a flood? I'm just telling
you to build a boat in your mind.
No easy fixes I'm afraid, but you can
eat the fish. Sequins make everything shine.

Thank you to my parents and sister for their continued support. Thank you, Stephanie, for being my best friend for nearly 20 years. Thank you, Christina, for seeing how alone I was that one Thanksgiving and being there these last 5 years. Thank you, James, for your constant encouragement, even when I am grumpy and don't want to hear it.

Thank you to The Coffeehouse Committee and Ozark Poetry Slam for introducing me to poetry. Thank you to the open mics and slam venues of Columbus, Ohio for making me a poet, and thank you to the MFA Program at Old Dominion University for allowing me the opportunity to study poetry.

Much appreciation to the following people and organizations who made spaces for me to write, perform, and engage with the literary community post-MFA: Patsy Asuncion, Tony Russell, James Cole, Stevie Edwards, Brittany Rogers, Kai Coggin, Rachel McKibbens, Michael Khandelwal, Andrea Gibson, The Poetry Barn, Gemini Ink, Winter Tangerine, The Muse, the Charlottesville Poetry Critique Circle, the monthly open mic at the Bridge Progressive Arts Initiative, and the Live Poets Society of Charlottesville, Virginia.

## Acknowledgements

"Vanishing Below the Waist" was previously published in *Requiem for a Doll* (ELJ Publications, 2015) and in *and for too long after* (Unsolicited Press, 2019).

"Eden" was previously published in *Requiem for a Doll* (ELJ Publications, 2015)

"Prophecy: A Recipe" appeared in *Peatsmoke*

"Poem in Which I Expand" appeared in *Breakwater Review*

"Blue Mud Dauber" appeared in *Slant*

"Vulvodynia" appeared in *Foundry*

"Everything is so okay" appeared in *Hematopoiesis*

"Street Corner Mermaid" appeared in *The Columbia Review*

"Unclogging the Shower Drain" appeared in *Ghost City Review*

"A Personal History of Bruxism" appeared in *Painted Bride Quarterly*

"Dream Lover" and "The Spectacle of Craving" appeared in *Third Wednesday*